DATE DUE

MRS. G. JOHNSON		
MRS. HILLMAN		
DEC 8 8 1997		
GAYLORD		PRINTED IN U.S.A.

The Night Workers

Alvin Schwartz

THE
NIGHT WORKERS

33181
Sc

Photographs by Ulli Steltzer

E. P. Dutton & Co., Inc.   New York

To the Night Workers

Contents

The Night Workers

Even as most of us sleep, there are men and women at work. In the glare of lights, in the darkness of shadows, with night all around them, they go about their jobs in places as different as fish markets and firehouses, tugboats and television studios. Although life would not be as pleasant or as safe without them, often their work and their world are unknown to day people.

Of course, the best way to meet night workers is by staying up with them. Let's suppose that it is late on a Monday afternoon, an hour or so before dark....

Everywhere at this time day workers are going home, crowding the streets and highways, filling the subways and the buses. In far smaller numbers, night workers have been returning to their jobs. This nurse, for example, will work until midnight in a children's ward. Then another nurse will take her place, remaining on duty until the day workers return.

It is now six o'clock. Work already has begun on tomorrow morning's newspaper. This rewrite man is taking notes as he talks to a reporter covering an important meeting downtown. When he hangs up, he will write a story that will appear in the newspaper's next edition about two hours from now. Elsewhere in the city room, stories on other events are being prepared. Still others clatter in on teletype machines from cities throughout the country and the world.

Three floors below, printers have just started their high-speed presses rolling with the first edition. By early tomorrow, when the sixth and last edition is run, 600 thousand newspapers will have been printed.

It is seven o'clock. Strange as it may seem, school has just begun. This is a class in writing. The teacher left her daytime job as an editor two hours ago, had dinner, then drove here. Her students did the same thing. They come to school two nights each week after work. Just as their children do, they listen, recite, try to finish their homework on time, and take tests. Many have returned to school because it helps them with their jobs. Others just want to learn. Over seventeen million adults go to school at night. As a result, so do a half million men and women who serve as their teachers.

Just a few minutes ago TV cameramen began filming this program of rock and roll music which is to be shown four days from now on 154 stations. Including this singer, there are over twenty performers. There also are more than seventy other night workers involved—directors, producers, stagehands, musicians, soundmen, and the cameramen. From the television screen, however, one would never know it.

You are looking into the hold of the freighter *American Crusader*. It is eight o'clock. Some 140 stevedores are working late to load the ship so that it can sail tonight for France. These men are storing packages of frozen meat. Canned goods, automobiles, washing machines, and other appliances also are being brought aboard.

Less than a mile away tons of vegetables have been arriving by truck and by train from farms all over the country. Now, the produce fills the sidewalks and the warehouses. Later tonight other trucks will cart it to the food stores.

It is nine o'clock. This research engineer is checking the results of an experiment conducted earlier today with models of an airplane that takes off and lands vertically but otherwise operates like other planes. As the models flew, they sent back radio signals which described how they performed. The signals were tape recorded. As the engineer plays the tape, the signals produce graphs on the screen and on the equipment behind him which give a picture of just what happened.

This fire station houses Engine Company 43, Ladder Company 9, and Rescue Squad 7. The fireman at the desk is listening to the fire alarms that come in from headquarters by bell and by loudspeaker. When an alarm is sounded for his district, he alerts the thirteen other firemen stationed here and they race for their trucks. It takes them but thirty-five seconds to get under way. So far tonight, they have been out once for a fire in a kitchen and once for a false alarm. No one knows what the rest of the night will bring.

Nearby, a water truck turns the streets a glistening black.

Elsewhere, an empty office building also is left glistening.

It is ten o'clock. Before an audience of nine hundred, the curtain has risen on the third act of *Mother Courage,* a play about a gypsy woman some four hundred years ago. You are watching from backstage. The man on the right is the stage manager. At the moment, his biggest job is seeing that the stage is properly lighted. The man on the left is helping him. Still other night workers help with sound effects, costumes, and props.

The zoo, on the other hand, is a quiet place at this hour. With but a single watchman to keep them company, most of the six hundred animals are asleep—or are about to go to sleep.

As the lion yawns, the conductor signals that it is time to leave. Journeying south from New York to New Orleans, his train has just made its first stop. When it arrives at 8 A.M. the day after tomorrow, it will have traveled 1,357 miles. Aboard are three hundred passengers and a crew of twenty-three, including the engineer, conductors and trainmen, waiters and cooks in the dining car, and porters in the sleeping cars.

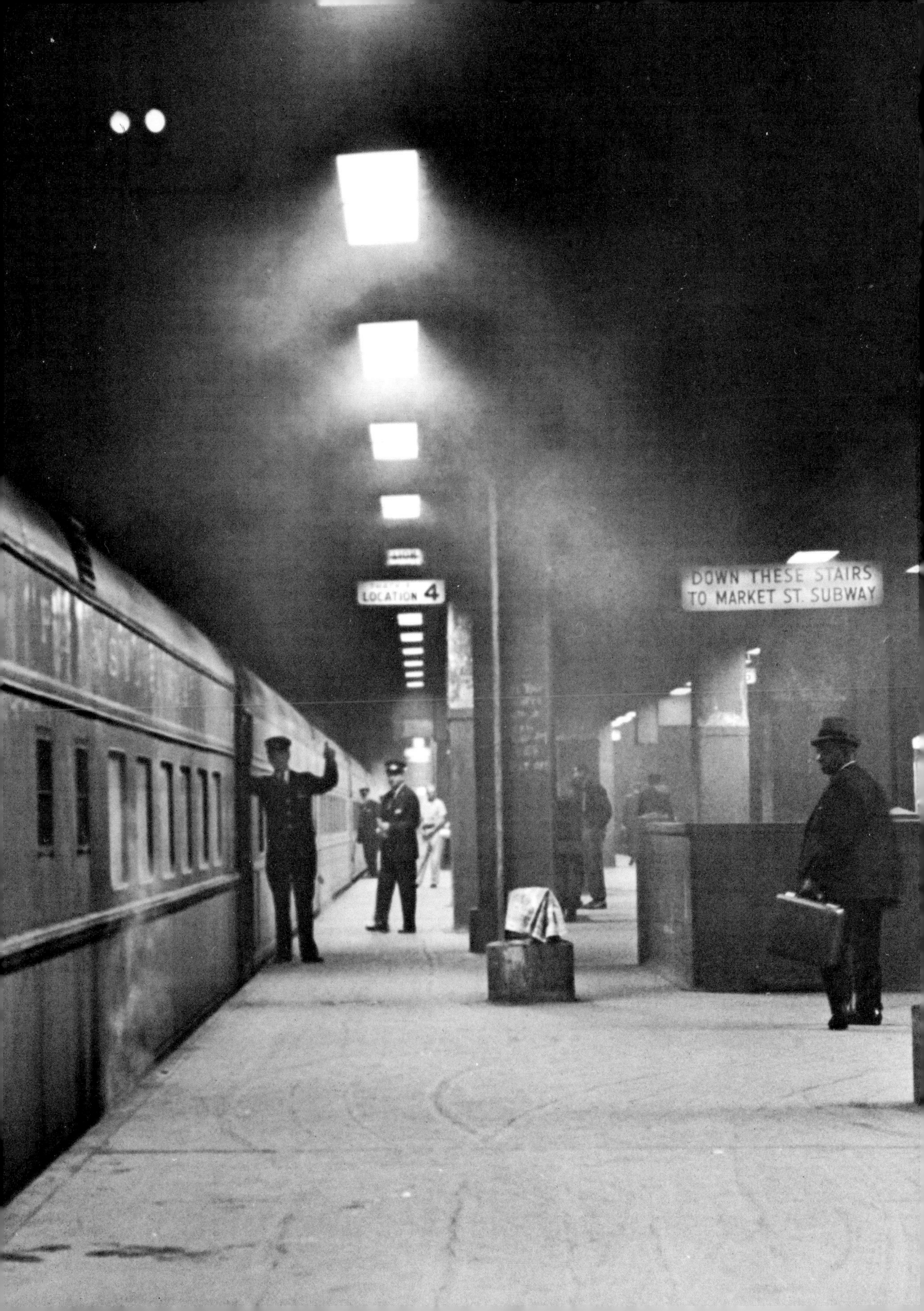
LOCATION 4
DOWN THESE STAIRS
TO MARKET ST. SUBWAY

Outside the train station a cab driver also prepares to leave.

Northeast of the city on a six-lane superhighway this bus driver and his forty-two passengers hurtle through the night toward Miami. He is the second of six drivers the bus will have on its 40-hour trip south from Montreal. The line of lights ahead is a bridge that crosses the highway.

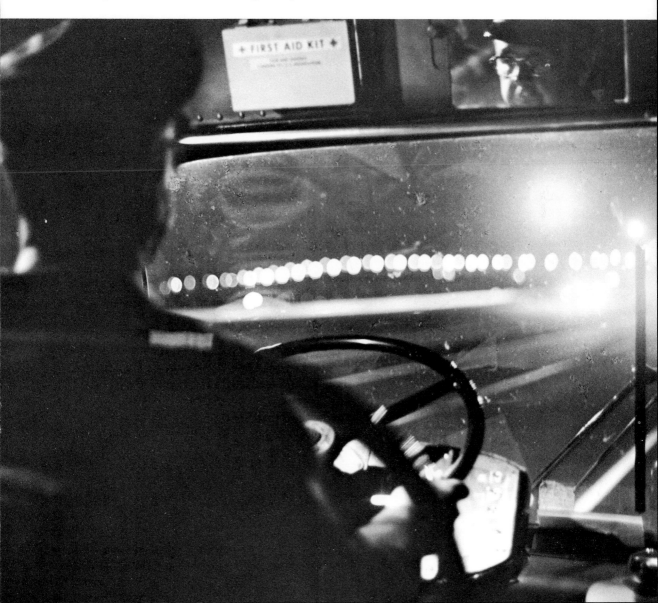

For the past fifteen minutes, this controlman has been guiding a 185,000-pound jet toward the airport. With the plane now close enough to make its approach, he is giving the pilot final landing instructions. "You are clear to land on Runway 4 Right. Wind 040 degrees at 17 knots...." Meanwhile, to the right where the streaks are, a plane has just left the ground. Each night, workers in this control tower help over two hundred planes to land and take off, guiding pilots along invisible air corridors toward or away from the runways. The radar screen above the controlman's head gives him a picture of what is going on in the air nearby.

It is eleven o'clock. Even now...

cooks carve...   waiters serve...

and students study.

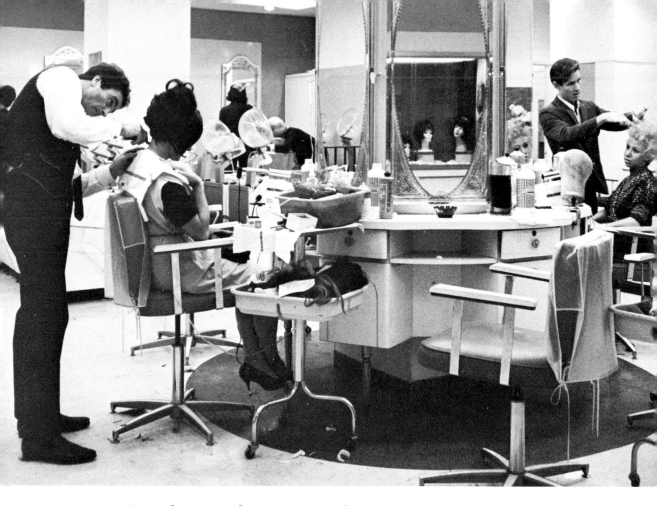

Hair dressers also are at work. Their customers are actresses, dancers, waitresses, and other night workers. To help them stay beautiful, this beauty parlor stays open all night.

It is almost midnight. The balloon the weatherman is about to release will carry the radio equipment he is holding as high as twenty-two miles. As it rises, the equipment will send back information on the weather at various altitudes. Balloons like this are sent up at midnight and at noon each day at five hundred weather stations around the world. The weather also is checked on the ground each hour at three thousand stations. All countries share in this information, whether or not they are friends.

Based on what he has found in his own area and what is happening elsewhere, the weatherman prepares his early morning forecast. Tomorrow? Fair and not quite so warm.

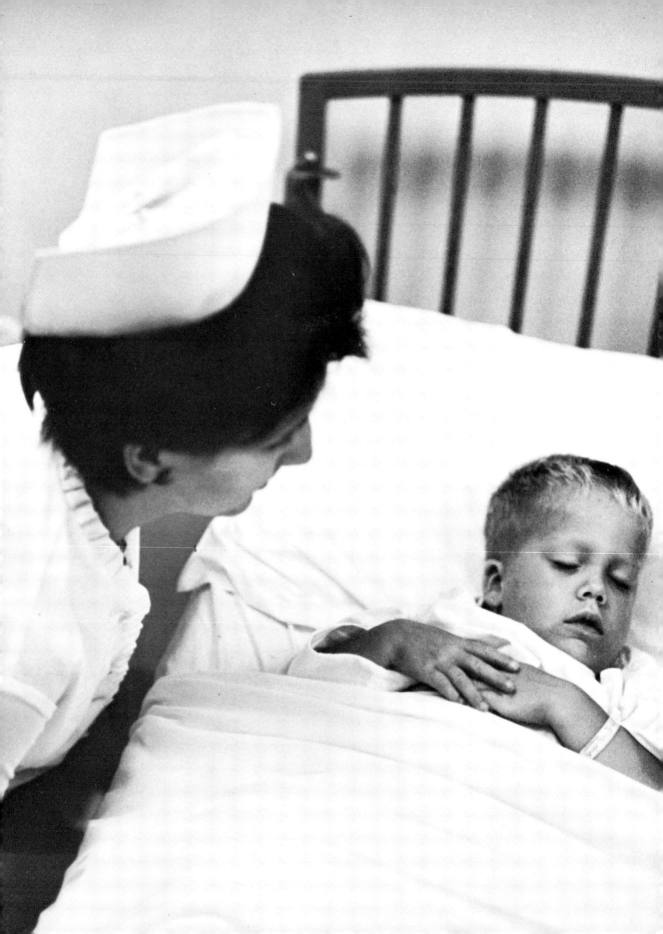

As this nurse was coming to work earlier today this four-year-old boy was brought to the hospital with a high fever. Now, halfway through the night, he sleeps. Elsewhere, nurses move quietly from room to room giving medicines, taking temperatures, comforting the sick and the lonely. In the emergency ward downstairs, two men injured when their car turned over are treated for cuts and bruises. In a dimly lighted room on the floor above, an old woman, almost ninety-three years old, dies in her sleep. At the other end of the building, a young mother gives birth to her first child, a girl she names Nancy Elizabeth.

People at home also need doctors and medicines. A short while ago the telephone rang in this all-night drug store. It was a doctor tending a sick boy. Would the druggist prepare a prescription and send it right over?

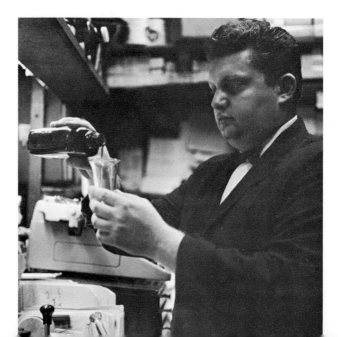

Steel also is being prepared at this hour. As the steelworker signals the operator of an overhead crane, 190 tons of molten iron are poured from this giant 14-foot ladle into an open-hearth furnace. After eight hours at 3,000 degrees, the iron becomes steel. Each night, the workers here turn out three thousand tons of this important metal.

It is now one o'clock. Over 2,500 men and women in this huge post office work at handling the nightly flood of mail into and out of the city. By morning, some five million letters and packages will have been brought in, sorted, and sent on their way. In post offices across the country tonight, 150 thousand night workers will move 140 million pieces of mail.

If your area code is 212 and your telephone number starts with 245 and you dial Operator about this time, one of these women may answer. If you have a different number, any one of thousands of other operators will help you. During the night fifty thousand are on duty. In this time, ninety million calls are made. Of course, most are handled by automatic equipment. The operator's job is to place calls when this equipment cannot be used and give information on telephone numbers. She also helps when doctors or police are needed, or in other emergencies. If service breaks down, fifty thousand repairmen also are on duty.

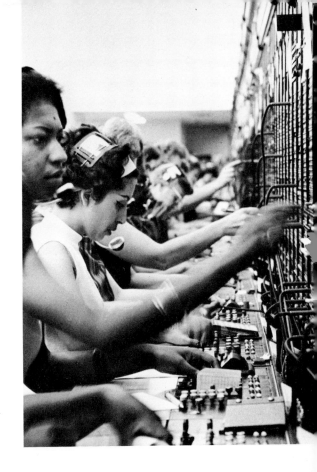

This telegram is being sent from New York to San Francisco. It is one of a hundred thousand that will be dispatched before morning. Many are from people who want to reach someone who doesn't have a phone. Many others are from businessmen who want their messages delivered early tomorrow. The telegram is being punched on a paper tape which is moving through a transmitter at the left. As the transmitter reads the tape, it sends electronic signals by way of Syracuse, New York, and Oakland, California, to a machine in San Francisco. The machine will print the message three minutes from now.

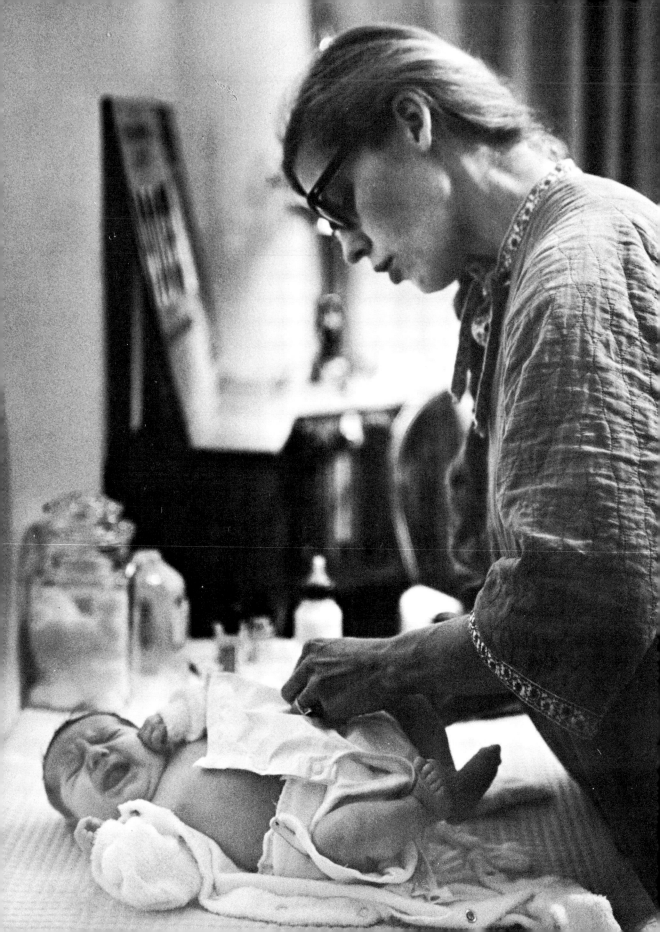

It is two o'clock. Crying, hungry, in need of fresh diapers, this month-old baby girl has just awakened. As a result, so has her sleepy mother who now is changing her and in a few minutes will feed her.

In a peaceful radio studio many miles way, this disc jockey plays records, reads the news, and talks about all sorts of things on a program called "Dawn Patrol." It is on from midnight to six o'clock in the morning. Who listens? Night workers, people who go to bed late, people who get up early, people who can't sleep, people with babies to change—altogether each night about 200 thousand men and women. A radio engineer is on the other side of the window. His job is to make sure that the program is loud enough and clear enough.

The man at the auxiliary wheel is the first mate of the tugboat *Eugene F. Moran*. Ahead in the darkness is the freighter *African Moon* outbound for Conakry, Monrovia, and Abidjan, West Africa. The tug is pushing the freighter from its berth into the harbor. Up ahead, another tug is pulling. Once in the harbor, the ship will head east into the ocean and the tugs will chug off to other assignments.

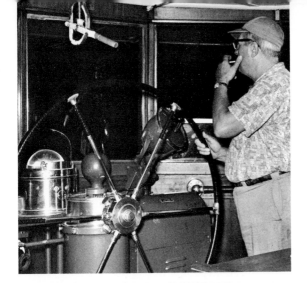

Captain

Chief Engineer

Deckhand

It takes eight men to operate a tugboat: the captain, his first mate, the chief engineer, the assistant engineer, the oiler, two deckhands, and a cook. The crew remains aboard as long as seventy-two hours at a time in all kinds of weather, docking and undocking ships, moving drydocks to where they are needed for ship repairs, hauling barges of oil, coal, and cement, and towing garbage scows.

This boxcar has just gone over the hump. Under the watchful eye of the brakeman riding on top, it is coasting down a gentle slope toward the classification area where freight trains are being made up. When the trains are complete, some will have 150 cars and extend for a mile and more. Which of the forty tracks ahead the car will use depends on which train it is joining.

The new trains grow out of other trains that arrive from the west with freight cars for this area. First, the old trains are broken up and their cars assigned to trains which will take them to their final destinations. Then, a switch engine like this one pushes the cars to the hump. As a car is released, a switchman throws a lever which sends it to the right track and the right train.

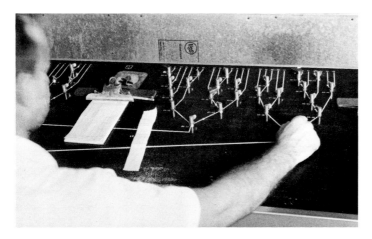

Over a million trucks also are on the move at this hour. When the driver finishes fastening the doors of this 50-foot tractor-trailer, he will head west from New Jersey to St. Louis with a 20-ton load of automobile parts, cloth, copper tubing, foodstuffs, and nuts and bolts. As he prepares to leave, dozens of other trucks are still being loaded.

It is three o'clock. You are looking into the operations room in one of the busiest of thirty police stations in this large city. It is where policemen make their reports and where persons suspected of crimes are officially arrested, or booked, before they stand trial in court. The man in the hat on the left has just been booked on a charge of stealing a wallet.

Throughout the city over a thousand policemen are on duty. Some patrol on foot, others by car. They report in each hour by telephone or by radio. In covering his beat, this foot patrol-man walks sixteen miles each night.

These men are luggers. They are moving sides of pork from a refrigerated truck to a refrigerated warehouse. Early each morning as the city's meat supply comes in, hundreds of luggers go to work. Along with pork, they move sides of beef, sides of lamb, boxes of chicken, even barrels of brains and barrels of bones. Once in the warehouse, the meat is cut to smaller sizes for use by butchers in the stores and by sausage makers and baloney makers.

Elsewhere at this hour there are music and dancing...

and phonograph records for sale.

REGISTRATION

CONFIRMED RESERVATIONS ONLY

Hotel clerks also are awake to sign in travelers who are late in arriving.

It is four o'clock. Today's supply of milk has begun to move from this giant refrigerator along a belt to delivery trucks outside.

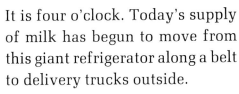

This driver delivers milk to stores, schools, hospitals, and restaurants. The cans contain bulk milk for baking and cooking and for machines from which milk is drawn by the glass. Earlier, workmen loaded sixty trucks that deliver milk directly to homes. From this one plant, almost fifty thousand quarts are distributed every morning.

Just about this time some night workers get hungry and head for a diner...and scrambled eggs and bacon...

or for a grocery and some ice cream or a delicatessen and a corned beef sandwich.

It is five o'clock. With morning but a few hours away, traffic into and out of the city is increasing and the toll-takers grow busier.

Downtown, this crew from the electric company is almost finished with the job of repairing a large underground steam pipe. All that remains is filling the deep hole and patching the street so that traffic will not be blocked. Throughout the night, five hundred men stand by to make such repairs.

Computers and the men who run them also are at work. This computer is figuring out how large a paycheck each of the two thousand workers in a factory will take home four days from now. The information it is using is on reels of tape you can see through the windows of the tape drives. One reel tells how much each worker is paid for an hour's work. Another tells how long he worked last week. Still another tells whether any of the work was of a special kind. It will take the computer ten minutes to do the arithmetic.

It is six o'clock. Wherever one turns in this sprawling, noisy water-front market, fish are heaped in glistening piles, the streets are wet with melted ice, and night workers with boots, ice picks, and evil-looking freight hooks move busily about. The fish have been arriving for hours in refrigerated trucks from fishing towns as far away as four hundred miles. They carry cod, mackerel, halibut, bass, snapper, flounder, tuna, even dogfish.

A set of scales is the most important equipment here. It is where the fish are weighed and the price is set. Most of the buyers are storekeepers and restaurant workers. However, a few are night workers seeking a tasty bargain on their way home—perhaps a striped bass like this one. Each morning almost a half million pounds of fish change hands.

An hour or so ago, the six bakers in this small Italian bakery began mixing and weighing the dough for the bread and rolls they bake each day. Right now, they are making long, narrow rolls for torpedo, hoagie, and submarine sandwiches. The bakers will turn out over three thousand rolls before they are finished. Tomorrow three thousand more will be needed.

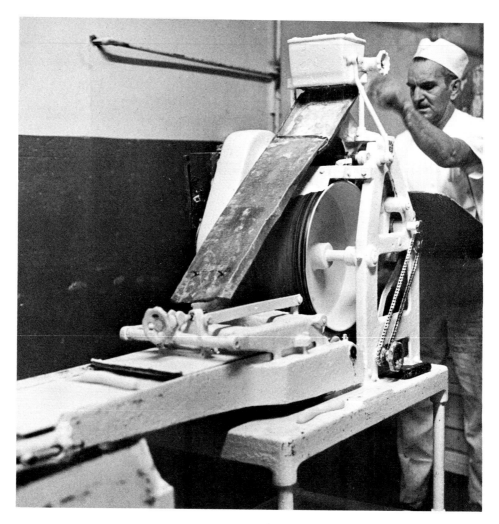

This baker is operating a machine that shapes the dough. If you look carefully, you will see a torpedo-to-be on the belt at the left.

After they are shaped, the rolls are placed on wooden boards and taken to the "proofer" room where they rise for half an hour.

Finally, they are placed inside the oven.

After a 20-minute ride on moving trays, they arrive back ready to eat.

When these men came to work, they found boxes and boxes of flowers waiting for them on the sidewalk. So did hundreds of other night workers in this marketplace. Now ugly gray shops up and down the street are filled with the color and the damp, sweet smell of roses, daisies, chrysanthemums, and dozens of other flowers. Soon messengers will carry them to florists throughout the city.

It is a quarter to seven. Night has begun to fade. This carrier boy has only a few more of his sixty papers to deliver. Then he will ride home, eat his breakfast, and try to get to school on time.

It is after eight. The sun is up. By bus, car, subway, and train the last of the night workers are heading for home.

Meanwhile, in a growing flood, day workers are returning. For them, for almost everyone else, the day has just begun.

How and where the photographs were taken

All of the photographs, with the exception of one, show real night workers on the job. The exception is the photograph of the night worker returning home. In this instance, the author, by this time a night worker in his own right, served as a model.

In almost every case, the photographs were made with only the light available and without flash guns and lamps. This was done to give as much of a sense as possible of what it is like to work at night.

Most of the photographs could have been made in any big city and its suburbs. Because the author and the photographer both live in the New York-Philadelphia area, the photographs were taken in those cities and also in Metuchen, New Brunswick, Franklin Township, Princeton, and Trenton, New Jersey, in Morrisville, Pennsylvania, and on the New Jersey Turnpike. The photographs were made in the locations listed below.

Day workers going home: Market and 15th Streets, Philadelphia, Pennsylvania.

Night worker returning to work: Mercer Hospital, Trenton, New Jersey.

Newspaper workers: Philadelphia *Inquirer*, Philadelphia, Pennsylvania.

Teacher: Scott Hall, Rutgers University, New Brunswick, New Jersey.

Television workers: National Broadcasting Company studio, RCA Building, Rockefeller Plaza, New York City, where the show "Hullabaloo" was being filmed. The singer is Dionne Warwick.

Stevedores: Hold of the United States Lines freighter *American Crusader,* Pier 54, foot of West 14th Street, New York City.

Produce market workers: Chambers and Washington Streets, New York City.

Research engineer: Forrestal Research Center, Princeton University, Princeton, New Jersey.

Fireman: Fire station, Market and 21st Streets, Philadelphia, Pennsylvania.

Street washer: Kennedy Boulevard and 15th Street, Philadelphia, Pennsylvania.

Janitor: Lobby, New York Life Insurance Company, East 27th Street near Madison Avenue, New York City.

Workers in a theatre: McCarter Theatre, Princeton, New Jersey.

Watchman at a zoo: Staten Island Zoo, Barrett Park, Staten Island, New York.

Train conductor: 30th Street Station, Pennsylvania Railroad, Philadelphia, Pennsylvania.

Cab driver: 30th Street Station, Philadelphia, Pennsylvania.

Bus driver: Greyhound Bus, New Jersey Turnpike, near Newark, New Jersey.

Airport controlman: Control Tower, John F. Kennedy Airport, New York City.

Workers in a restaurant: La Fonda del Sol, West 50th Street near Avenue of the Americas, New York City.

Students: Firestone Library, Princeton University, Princeton, New Jersey.

Workers in beauty parlor: Larry Matthews Beauty Salon, 118 West 57th Street, New York City.

Steel worker: United States Steel Corporation's Fairless Works, Morrisville, Pennsylvania.

Nurse: Children's ward, Mercer Hospital, Trenton, New Jersey.

Pharmacist: Kaufman Pharmacy, Lexington Avenue at East 49th Street, New York City.

Weathermen: Weather Bureau Station, Hangar 11, John F. Kennedy Airport, New York City.

Post office workers: General Post Office, 8th Avenue at West 33rd Street, New York City.

Telephone operators: New York Telephone Company, 435 West 50th Street, New York City.

Telegram operator: Western Union office, 1440 Broadway, New York City.

Workers at a truck terminal: Eastern Freight Terminal, U.S. 1, Metuchen, New Jersey.

Workers in a railroad freight yard: Pennsylvania Railroad Freight Yard, Morrisville, Pennsylvania.

Tugboat workers: Aboard the *Eugene F. Moran* in New York Harbor off Pier 35, Brooklyn, New York.

Luggers in a meat market: West 14th and Washington Streets, New York City.

Mother: Coppermine Road, Franklin Township, New Jersey.

Disc jockey: Radio Station WIP, 19th and Walnut Streets, Philadelphia, Pennsylvania.

Policemen: Operations room, 6th District Police Station, 11th and Winter Streets; police beat, 8th and Arch Streets, both Philadelphia, Pennsylvania.

Jazz musicians: Eddie Condon's, 330 East 56th Street, New York City. Peanuts Hucko's Dixieland All-Stars are on the bandstand.

Worker in a record shop: Colony Record Center, 1671 Broadway, New York City.

Hotel Clerk: Hotel Commodore, Lexington Avenue and East 42nd Street, New York City.

Workers at a milk plant: The Borden Company, 234 North Broad Street, Trenton, New Jersey.

Workers in a diner: Colonial Diner, U.S. 1, near Princeton, New Jersey.

Supermarket clerk: Smiler's, 850 Seventh Avenue, New York City.

Toll-taker: Verrazano-Narrows Bridge, Staten Island, New York.

Electric company workers: Near 64 Fulton Street, New York City.

Computer operator: Computer Service Center, International Business Machines Corporation, Time-Life Building, West 50th Street and Avenue of the Americas, New York City.

Fish market workers: Fulton and South Streets, New York City.

Bakers: Rossi's Baking Company, 24 North Stockton Street, Trenton, New Jersey.

Flower market workers: Mutual Cut Flower Company, 46-48 West 28th Street, New York City.

Newspaper carrier boy: Texas Avenue and Princeton Pike, Trenton, New Jersey. The paper is the Trenton *Trentonian*.

Night worker going home: North Clinton Avenue and Dewey Avenue, Trenton, New Jersey.

Day workers returning to work: Market and 15th Streets, Philadelphia, Pennsylvania.

Acknowledgments

I am particularly grateful to the night workers pictured in this book and to their organizations for their splendid help and remarkable patience.

ALVIN SCHWARTZ